Warren Sumner Barlow

Immortality Inherent in Nature

Warren Sumner Barlow

Immortality Inherent in Nature

ISBN/EAN: 9783743313101

Manufactured in Europe, USA, Canada, Australia, Japa

Cover: Foto ©ninafisch / pixelio.de

Manufactured and distributed by brebook publishing software
(www.brebook.com)

Warren Sumner Barlow

Immortality Inherent in Nature

.

IMMORTALITY

INHERENT IN NATURE.

BY

WARREN SUMNER BARLOW,

AUTHOR OF "THE VOICES," AND OTHER POEMS.

One chain of causes and effects
Encircles Nature's vast domain;
One universal voice proclaims
All is, and ever will remain.
See Canto 5th, 6th Verse.

"All are but parts of one stupendous whole
Whose body Nature is, and God the soul."
—POPE.

NEW YORK:

FOWLER & WELLS CO.,

753 BROADWAY.

1885.

TROW'S
PRINTING AND BOOKBINDING COMPANY,
NEW YORK.

To those who doubt immortal life,
    And feed upon the husks of fate ;
Who dare not trust their fondest hopes,
    These lines in love we dedicate.

CONTENTS.

IMMORTALITY.

"GOD IS ALL IN ALL."

ETERNAL Father—Life Divine,
   Thou boundless Evermore;
O teach this feeble erring soul
   Thy goodness to adore.

Thy watchful care with unseen hands
   Moulds and directs the whole,
While universal order reigns
   By Thy divine control.

The music of the rolling spheres,
  Attuned and held by Thee,
Forever thrills the universe
  With silent harmony.

Unnumbered families of worlds
  Their yearly circuits run,
While borne upon the wings of light
  Around their parent sun.

Athwart the heaven's etherial dome,
  Where angel feet have trod,
The panorama brings to light
  The alphabet of God.

All Nature speaks with countless tongues
  The language of each sphere,
Whose voice of harmony is heard
  By every list'ning ear.

And though we fail to comprehend
   The earth's minutest grains,
The central heart of Nature lives
   And flows in all their veins.

O who can fathom Nature's depths,
   Or trace her trackless rounds,
Whose secret seals their vigils keep,
   Unknown by lines or bounds?

A fraction of Infinitude
   If measured or defined,
Would circumscribe the boundless realms
   Of the Eternal Mind.

All *central,* no *circumference,*
   If Nature hath no bounds;
She neither can be *more,* nor *less,*
   In her unending rounds.

Thus with Infinitude of *life*,
    Whose life " is all in all ; "
If death annihilates a part,
    Omnipotence may fall.

But God—the universal Life—
    His life to all secures,
Which must extend to all extent,
    While God Himself endures.

His boundless being binds the whole,
    That all, His life may share ;
Encircled in His arms of love,
    All feel His tender care.

One life embodied in all forms ;
    One limitless control ;
One chain of many golden links,
    Unites and binds the whole.

One universal law of love
  Is seen in all we trace;
One vast Infinitude is held
  By God's divine embrace.

O Thou unknown, yet known to all;
  Though found, art ever sought;
We feel Thou art the central source
  Of Being, Life, and Thought!

CANTO I.

THE SOURCE OF THOUGHT IS ETERNAL.

Think not that conscious souls will sleep
    Forever in a dreamless night ;
While matter gross forever lives,
    And moves in pleasant paths of light.

As rivers, with resistless force,
    All carve their pathway to the sea ;
So restless man forever yearns
    For blissful immortality.

Unlike the rivers ocean bound,
   Which mingle in the rolling strife,
The souls that flood the stream of time,
   Forever crave a conscious life.

The aspirations of the soul
   Are living germs that will mature ;
And fondest hopes are promises
   Of golden fruitage, made secure.

The rocks that held all forms of life,
   In their primeval solitude,
Have clothed the earth in rich attire,
   In every zone and longitude.

Their massive brows, long turned to dust,
   Display their type on nature's page ;
Whose precious gems, unscathed by time,
   Outlive all forms from age to age.

The diamond, with its eyes of fire,
  Beholds its kindred forms decay;
In youthful vigor, undefiled,
  It lives while ages wend their way.

Then must the germs of life and thought
  Commingle with a senseless clod,
While inborn Hope for endless years
  Is thus a counterpart of God?

If transient rocks contain a gem
  That lives while forms that held it fall,
May not our throbbing heart-strings hold
  A prize more precious far than all?

If conscious memory outlives
  Each mortal form, of seven years span,
And holds the record of them all,
  Why not survive the age of man?

The answer lives in every soul,
  Responsive to our heart's desires,
For on Love's altar Hope was born,
  And kindled her eternal fires.

Can being doubt its end and aim,
  Whose thoughts have lived from age to age,
And will survive the flight of time,
  On memory's immortal page ?

Can thus a feeble, fleeting soul—
  The short-lived tenant of the earth,
With hopes like bubbles, soon to burst,
  To an immortal thought give birth ?

If thus Effect outweighs its Cause,
  The " Great First Cause," in dread alarm,
Beholding now His waning power,
  May yield His weak and palsied arm.

If Cause doth not survive Effect,
    Or bows submissive to its call,
All thought and substance, left to chance,
    To chaos soon must fade and fall.

When Time turns back his dial-plate,
    And Nature countermands her laws,
And Darkness craves the beams of light,
    Effects may triumph over Cause.

Till then, the source of thought will live,
    And still retain its life divine,
Where age adorns immortal youth,
    As conscious souls more brightly shine.

A trio of eternities,
    The present, future, and the past,
Will bear us on their central waves,
    And doubly crown our hopes at last!

CANTO II.

Cause proclaims its changeless purpose
  In the language of Effects,
Universal and eternal,
  Which the universe reflects.

Interwoven through the ages,
  All Effects must ever last ;
Hold the present, shape the future,
  Crown with glory all the past.

From all star-lit constellations,
   To the mote which naught detects,
All, except the Cause of Causes,
   Lives forever in Effects.

.

Then, must conscious life and being
   Languish on the verge of thought,
Strangle every aspiration,
   And forever come to naught?

Must the soul, that crowns creation—
   Essence of immortal truth—
Grand Effect above all others,
   Not survive its wayward youth?

When unending space is bounded,
   And all systems come to naught,
And eternity no longer
   Bears the record of a thought,

Then Effect, devoid of being,
    Cause may nevermore rehearse
The Eternal Power and Wisdom
    That ordained the universe.

But Effect will ride forever
    In the chariot of Cause
Driven by inherent forces,
    Guided by unerring laws.

Cradled in the mist of ages,
    Borne upon the breath of time,
Man will reach, through love and wisdom,
    An immortal height sublime.

CANTO III.

To doubt Effect, we question God,
    With all his attributes divine,
Whose rays of wisdom, truth and love,
    On all his works forever shine.

Cause must determine all Effects,
    And Love obeys its wise behest;
Then, as the "Great First Cause" directs,
    All are, and ever will be, blest.

Free Agency and Sovereignty
　Are partners in a common cause,
To elevate immortal man,
　Through knowledge of unchanging laws.

But every soul is free to act,
　Within the circuit of its sphere ;
Where all, in Nature's ample school,
　Will learn God's purpose to revere.

And man alone of all the tribes
　That tread the earth, or beat the air,
Is born with freedom's armor on,
　And must life's conflicts ever share.

His sphere of freedom, though defined
　By walls that limit self-control,
Will widen and extend its bounds,
　As wisdom doth expand the soul.

But for the tribes *below* mankind,
 Instinctive wisdom holds the reins,
And safely guides and governs all,
 By laws that bind them with its chains.

The countless beasts that roam the fields,
 And quench their thirst from laughing rills,
Select from earth's extended plains,
 The food their nature best distills.

The birds are made to build their nests,
 The first as perfect as the last ;
To swell their breasts with cheerful song,
 The changeless song of ages past.

The bee invites us to behold
 The wonders of its matchless skill ;
No hand can mould its waxen cups,
 Much less from flow'ry petals fill.

The spider spins and weaves its web,
    Each strand with almost countless threads,
Whose lines by genius are defined,
    On which it mounts and safely treads.

The ant a lesson gives to all,
    Of patience, industry, and care ;
The insects of the vasty deep,
    That plant the coral mountains there,

Proclaim, with all the instinct tribes,
    In language man may understand,
That wise design pervades the whole—
    That power divine is in command.

Thus all these tribes are wisely led
    By hands unseen the world around,
No path diverging turns their course,
    No bar to intercept is found.

Like plants and trees, they come and go,.
   Like grass and flowers, they fade and die,
Yet leave their problems still unsolved,
   Which none can fathom or deny.

But man at birth is weak and frail—
   A helpless, thankless, hopeless soul,
Yet reason holds a gift divine—
   The power to rise, through self-control.

Though far more helpless than the brute,
   He holds within his baby hand
The golden keys that will unlock
   The choicest treasures of the land.

Thus man alone, of all the earth,
   By God endowed is thus made free;
That through the endless rounds of life,
   He may *himself*, forever be.

Forever learning, yet unlearned;
   Forever rising, still to rise;
Forever living, still to live
   Where naught but pain and sorrow dies.

This power of choice, bequeathed to man
   By God's immutable decree,
As part of His revokeless plan,
   Is lasting as eternity.

To limit freedom to this life,
   Eternal problems to rehearse,
Then chain us to the wheels of fate,
   And march us through the universe.

Revokes the purposes of God,
   And limits law to time and place;
Forever bars the doors of hope,
   And ends the progress of the race.

Progression is our end and aim,
    Revokeless as the days and years;
Unlimited by wisdom's ways,
    Eternal as the rolling spheres.

In this progressive school, the soul
    In search of happiness, will learn
In time, or in eternity,
    To choose the right, the wrong to spurn.

The penalties that lie in wait
    For all who ever go astray
Are danger-signals in our path,
    To turn us from the downward way,

Until our dormant souls arouse,
    By Love's divine, chastising hand;
Imparting lessons all must heed,
    And cannot fail to understand.

But Love invites us to explore
    The beauties of her chosen way ;
Where all, by Wisdom's holy light,
    Will learn her precepts to obey.

The restless freedom of the soul,
    Though shores define its inland sea,
Will span the narrow bounds of time,
    To oceans of eternity.

Free Agency and Sovereignty,
    So nurture and direct the mind,
That knowledge, through experience,
    Will crown with glory all mankind.

Thus all will rise by force of will—
    Free agent of our dormant powers ;
Inspired by Courage, led by Hope,
    It guides us through our darkest hours,

Until, triumphant, every soul
    Will harmonize with Nature's laws—
The standard of the universe;
    Whose author, is the "Great First Cause."

O Source of wisdom, truth, and love,
    Teach us Thy precepts to obey,
That we may not retard our flight
    By errors that beset the way.

CANTO IV.

DESIGN VERSUS CHANCE.

Design—primordial of law—
  The universal foe to chance—
The thought, that moulds and guides the whole,
  Is fashioned by omnipotence.

Unnumbered voices all proclaim,
  Through Wisdom, Truth, and Love Divine,
That restless, tireless, endless spheres,
  Are all propelled through wise design,

Design, must have a primal source,
 As all effects must follow cause ;
And he who doubts these golden rules.
 Must question well-established laws.

Our mortal forms inwrought with care,
 Each part adapted to the whole,
Dispel the very dreams of Chance,
 And glorify divine control.

But should disease and early death
 Extend their cold, relentless hands,
And leave us lonely in our grief,
 By breaking love's unsullied bands,

We might in sorrow, grief and pain
 Almost disown the power supreme,
And, with a vague, bewildered sense,
 Behold in all an empty dream.

But if our vision could expand,
    And view the breadth of Nature's rule,
We might conclude too oft we were
    Rebellious pupils from her school.

All pain or death, not crowned with age,
    Are accidents in life's career—
Are shoals adown the stream of time,
    Which all avoid who safely steer.

To entertain unholy thoughts
    And clothe them with their kindred deeds,
We crush the budding flowers of hope,
    And cultivate pernicious weeds.

Immutable are Nature's laws,
    Regardless of our weal or woe,
And though we scatter tares or wheat,
    "We must all gather what we sow."

Thus Justice poises every deed,
  Though men, or nations, rise or fall,
And Time will vindicate the truth
  That love divine is all in all.

If naught creates, controls, presides,
  The being, end, and aim of man
Are but the vague behests of Chance,
  Devoid of purpose, thought or plan.

And Nature, with reluctant hands,
  Her treasures undirected yields;
While Hope invites us to regale
  On barren and forbidden fields.

If Law were severed from Design,
  Chaotic worlds, in wild affright,
Would dim the battlements of time,
  And shroud infinitude with night.

I fain, with homely reverie,
    Would, by a simple thought, explain
That which my oft-bewildered pen
    May here disguise in its refrain.

Were billiards played without design,
    Its balls by law, through *Chance* would roll,
Such heedless Chance, in vague command,
    Would send confusion through the whole.

But let *Design* enforce the law,
    As skilful hands direct the play,
And law, no longer ruled by Chance,
    No ball need ever go astray.

Thus Nature heeds the silent power,
    That through infinitude abounds,
Where wise Design controls the law
    That swings all systems in their rounds.

Through trackless paths their measured flight
   Is guided by unerring skill ;
As moments counted will define
   The time and place that each must fill ;

While weary thought without a poise,
   To take the burden from her wings,
In search of chaos, Chance, or bounds,
   Returning message never brings.

Through Nature's vast unsolved domain,
   The crowning purpose of the whole,
The life, for which all else was made,
   Is centred in the human soul.

Design—the central source of power—
   The thought that fashions every plan—
The crowning jewel of the soul,
   Is only found in God, and man.

Design hath bridged from shore to shore
    The dark veiled chasm of despair,
On which immortal life hath reared
    Her temple so divinely fair.

Though nurtured in the dusty garb
    Of time's unsought, unsolved career,
Yet, with Jehovah's Fatherhood,
    Why grope in darkness, doubt, and fear ?

As this our sun gave birth to worlds,
    From which our system was set free,
All fashioned from his elements,
    Eternal in their entity ;

So hath the central Source of thought,
    From all its attributes divine,
Bequeathed immortal life to man,
    To crown with glory all Design.

O who can comprehend the power
    That poises systems in their flight,
That holds creation in its hands,
    And floods the universe with light?

Yet all this wond'rous power is Love,
    Portrayed in one stupendous plan,
In one expression, all expressed—
    Eternal happiness for man.

O Father, in whose love we live,
    Whose life in all is love divine,
We would obey Thy holy will,
    And glorify Thy wise design.

CANTO V.

HOPE OF THE SOUL.

Sweet Hope, thy star will yet adorn
  The zenith of a cloudless sky,
Whose bright effulgence never wanes,
  Whose aspirations never die.

Eternal progress rends the vail,
  And gives to Reason ample scope,
Whose massive brow, and measured step,
  Is ballast to the wings of Hope.

Each soul a finite god will rise
   Majestic in its entity;
Maturing by its inborn strength,
   Coeval with Eternity.

Shall forms of dust that clothe the soul
   Outlive a thought that moves the world,
That times the circuit of the spheres
   Which through infinitude are whirled?

Nay, man, thy noble end and aim
   Are not disarmed by feeble dust;
Then give Inspiring Hope her wings,
   For while *God* lives, in Him *we* must.

One chain of Causes and Effects
   Encircles Nature's vast domain;
One universal voice proclaims,
   All *is,* and ever *will* remain!

"THE VOICES,"

BY WARREN SUMNER BARLOW.

This work of nearly 300 pages (price $1.00) has now reached its eleventh edition.

TESTIMONIALS.

From the many critical notices and reviews of "The Voices," we have only room for a few brief extracts:

Judge Baker, of New York, in his elaborate review of "The Voices," says: "Considered in the light of a controversial or didactic poem, it is without an equal in contemporaneous literature—the birth of an audacious mind, and is destined to excite greater and more wide-encircling waves of sectarian agitation than any anti-credal work ever published."

Professor S. B. Brittan, in his able review of the work, says: "In 'The Voice of Nature' the author gives us a clearer insight into his own views of the material world, of human nature and

God.   He has a rational philosophy of the relations of mind
and matter, and his theology is at once natural and charitable.
He recognizes one God everywhere, present alike in the physical
world and in His moral universe.   The God he adores, and his
strong faith in the goodness that rules the world, are clearly re-
vealed and forcibly expressed in the following paraphrastic and
poetical rendering of a beautiful passage in the Sermon on the
Mount:

> " Will He who hears the ravens when they cry,
> Mock and deride thee when no hope is nigh?
> Will he who clothes the lilies of the field,
> That neither toil, nor spin, nor raiment yield;
> Who feeds the fowls that never reap nor sow—
> Extends His watchful care where'er they go;
> Will He who clothes the grass which is to-day,
> While all its beauty quickly fades away,
> Forget His image—His immortal child?
> Is he alone derided and defiled,
> Or left to tread the downward thoroughfare,
> With Satan to bewilder and ensnare,
> And urge him on to death and dark despair?
> ' O, ye of little faith,' let reason sway :
> Are not your souls more precious far than they?"

William H. Burleigh, a well-known author and poet, in one of
his contributions to the Chicago *Evening Post*, thus speaks of the
author, and "The Voices:" "That he is a bold, earnest man,
with very pronounced opinions, that he has a combative and in-
cisive way of stating those opinions, and that, below all seeming
antagonism to the letter of old creeds, he accepts the spirit of the
new dispensation, his book furnishes abundant evidence.   His
verse is generally characterized by vigor, and at times glides with
a true rhythmic flow, and rings with a genuine poetic harmony."

www.ingramcontent.com/pod-product-compliance
Lightning Source LLC
Chambersburg PA
CBHW032140080426
42733CB00008B/1145